POEMS

MARCIA NARDI

D1364366

NEW POETRY SERIES

ALAN SWALLOW, Denver

Library of Congress Cataloging in Publication Data

Nardi, Marcia.
    Poems.

    Reprint of the 1956 ed. published by A. Swallow, Denver,
in series: New poetry series.
    I. Title.
[PS3527.A5P6   1975]   811'.5'4   79-179816
ISBN 0-404-56016-4
       0-404-56000-8 (SET)

The New Poetry Series

Reprinted by arrangement with
The Swallow Press Inc.
Copyright © 1956 by Marcia Nardi
First AMS edition published in 1975
AMS Press Inc. 56 E. 13th St.
New York, N.Y. 10003

Manufactured in the USA

145003

ACKNOWLEDGMENT

Some of these poems have appeared in *New Directions,*
Commentary, Botteghe Oscure, Poetry: A Magazine of
Verse, and *American Scholar.*

The author wishes to thank the Edward MacDowell
Association for the opportunity to write some of these
poems.

CONTENTS

OCTOBER HOUSE GUEST

And now you are all going abroad
You to Saint Jean de Luz
And to Fontainebleau you and Menton,
And you with the numerous friends there
To Italy's many suns
Now that autumn has come
While I here at home
Must go down with the chipmunk to the hole
That is there again this year
In the native land of my flesh-and-bone.

You will send me postcards
Of the Louvre and Coloseum
If I should send you one
You would say "Come,
My cousins can put you up
My aunt has extra rooms—
You are not Tom Thumb."

But the place where I shall winter
Here at home
Is not so small at all
When you consider how small my soul has become
Measured beside this new grief
This little low moan just born

Which is only little
And only low
When I think of the Prado's ceilings
As St. Peter's over you,
But very big really . . . too spacious really for keeping
    warm,

When you think of the size of the chipmunk
And the size of my soul
And also
Of the size of the mole
Who could do with a tinier niche than the one
That will house me again this year, the mind's paths
    gone,
Here in that dark country where the same thrust
Makes no different burrow
Whether love's or lust's.

PASTORAL SCENE

Astray, I walked into the calendar picture
Of the grazing cow and calf and the sheep
And anyone could have left me then—
Lover or friend—and I would not have missed him,
One of the figures stretched there on the lawn
Having turned so easily into me.

What did I walk out of? A siesta? A play?
My life it was, my time, the scenery of my day to day
As Breughel might have painted them, or Sisley,
Or even Giotto . . . being less far away
Than the calendar picture I walked into
From the mirror of my within
And the landscape of my outward way.

And I saw and loved again
The Noah's Ark beasts of my childhood,
So identically these . . . this cow, this sheep,
And as far removed from the real, coached and guided,
As the literal meanings of words from speech.

My back was to the automobiles
But I felt them carry off
The canvases for centuries hung
Over the cow of my ark
And an apple tree that resisted
Obeisance to Ingres as well as Braque,
And imprisoned there in the calendar picture I found
Odysseus with the fetters lost
And greenness the sound.

ALONE WITH A POEM

I

The idea you innocently play with—
Indifferent to what it may lead to
Or, rather, not thinking about it much—
Touching it, brushing against it . . . the stranger
You sit near at a party
And at your leisure, for an hour's past-time,
May see again . . . or the child
Still young enough to take upon your knee and fondle,
Foot-loose—your nostrils lowered
Over a road-side rose . . . .

How these gold virginal moments,
Like those recaptured Edens
When the body wakes from sleep before the mind,
Must fade into the distance
All their myth's brightness
Misted and shadowy,

When the child, a year older,
Turns flower to lodestar

Or into your sun and air
Grows the attractive stranger,

When your idea
Thrusting upon you an unmade poem, makes
The true rape God's of Mary.

II

Alone with a poem
Its pulse still homeless
And for its marrow no bones

And when like Adam
You are asked to provide them
Groping for your own.

Your thought running from you
Just outside your window
At your call turning but running on
Because you have no face yet
Because it does not know you
Because you are the original Thurston
Waiting
For a world of his own making
In order to be born,
The creator creating to be created
The womb within a womb—

Not as the prisoners of islands
Nor a monastery's lonely ones,
As the dying only
Miles from the arms they lie in
With your poem alone
But towards those arms flowing
Not flowing from—

Alone with a poem
Its bones not formed yet
Its pulse-beat awaiting a wrist
As if love came on Campion rhythms to find you
And you raised up phantom lips for its kiss—

This loafing, this terror,
This agony,
This is the first of the forbidden pleasures
This is the chief of the eleven Commandments'

Interdits

And how you envy the committers
Of theft and adultery,
And all the sweaters
In mines and in factories
With their double
Sabbath-day pay . . .
These how you envy!

What holds you then? What holds you?
Why not go? Why do you stay?
What binds you to this fire, half snow—
To this Gethsemane?
If you cannot answer
At least you know
That the Croesuses and Caesars
Have not everything to do
With the Sudras of all centuries.

CONCERT

It played the people—
It played the dark head near the fair one
It played the cloaked arm next to the bare one,
And the curve of cheeks
And the slope of shoulders . . .
This was the piece the trio played.
When the soft pedal came
That paunch there, faded
And the pianist played only the beautiful forehead,
And the tilt of throats with the furrows muted
Was what the cello and violin played—
They played the gestures and positions
Of human boughs and flowers and leafage
Far from their lathes and from their spinning,
They played the people as they listened,
And when the flute joined in the flutist
Is what it played—
It played the soloist's youth and beauty,
The slender flute played her slender bosom
And her slender waist and her arms like tendrils
Upon a vine forever green.
If the dead could have been there
It might have played
Onto their bones the round flesh again.

WINTER LANDSCAPE

In no hot August were ever stiller
The dark heads of the pine trees
Not a hair stirred
Not a loose lock lifted
And without a shiver
Upon the earth's white bloodless bosom
The motionless shadows of the bare trunks lay
As if on fur or woolen.

No bed of daisies or white alyssum
Was ever whiter than that snow
The moon new-dipped in fresh gold plating
Gleamed in the brightness that from below
Made the cloudless sky so light
Only three stars showed.

Nothing moved
Except a lantern in the distance
Nothing barked
Or chirped or whispered
And on a path too narrow for two
Only your own frozen footprints
Pointed the way to the woodshed
And came right back to you.

It was a night to gaze at from the window
It was no night to go out into
Unless you could stop all thinking, laughing, dreaming
All hoping, caring, and all grieving
And stand there—
Another motionless pine-tree in the snow.

COUNTRY LETTER

I write to you from the country—
Though the pavements have followed me here
And the florists stand by for the rose
If the winds of a few weeks ago
Had slipped through these hills
Had cut straight through
Them sideways
Slicing them off slicing away
My breasts like their ache for you
I could come home to myself at least
To my sister grief
To the arms of Dido alive again
In the mirror of my pain
If not to you, my love, if not to you.

But faith, I know,
My faith of a year ago
When your absence not yet was real to my veins
Saw this land through
Those days when the March winds blew
The last armor away of the heart's protective snow
And these valleys now
Gray still and leafless
Even today in April—these
Are the vowels . . . the vowel sounds
In the words with the deep soft "u,"
The words with the vulva—deep as it—
And the feminine armpits shaved and smooth
Like "love," my Love,
And the word tabooed,
And waiting—as only women wait—
For God, in creating the world, to use.

In their prayer for greenness
I'd say that Heloise and her letters were here
And she who died in Portugal,
But too hopeful for prayer
These valleys and these hills.

I write to you from the country
But when I touch—in exile from your touch—
A shrub or tree
And sink my naked feet into the thawed-out fields
My hand to my hand is China far away
And to my heart my heart an ice-locked sea
And always the prison matron's watchful eye
Goes with us to the bathing rooms
And haunts the darkness as we climb
Into our separate beds at night to sleep.

Not only my life is lost and betrayed
But my death also
Like that of mummies
Or those who in cities see
From a hospital window
Even their Potter's Field filled in with bricks—
The pavements have followed me here
But I write to you from the country.

WEIGHTED WITH LACK

My mind said *giddy-up* all day
But only time moved
Only time went away
The dray
Horse of my nothingness
Stayed.

Though morning and noon and the whole afternoon
To my *giddy-up* galloped away,
Weighted with lack—
The void in my loins
Overloading its back,
It did not go
It did not stir
It only strove and strained,
And the sun went down
And the wind blew
While I remembered the *whoa*
Of long ago
When light with having,
Of time and the wind and all things
I was the flow.

AND I KNEW THE BODY A SEA

I

Out there on the moor
At your own door
For twenty years, Cathy,
Have you waited
Begging to be let in?
I too I said
I have knocked at my ribs
And at my limbs
And at my head
I have knocked at my loins
And at my breast—
At all the dark shutters and walls
Wildly I've knocked and have called
Those are my guts there inside
Those are my lungs, that heart-beat is mine—
This is my home, I have cried,
Let me in . . . .
For twenty years
With no roof and no floor
Out in the cold, at the very door
Of my self
I have waited and called
Like you, Catherine.

And not on the moor
But behind sealed doors
Locked not out but in
For twenty years have you waited,
Penelope, for the wind?
I too my body moaned—

For my self to come home
To steal in past my bones
For twenty years have I waited,
Yea, though I fed
The usurpers of my absent lord's throne
Though I listened and hoped when my liver and gall
And my belly and all
My three billion cells
And the hairs on my head
Glibly promised and begged
We will be your self
If your self does not come,
Without one I heeded.

Did you hear that, Cathy?
Did you hear what my body said?
Or of Penelope have you never read?
It was Penelope I called to
Cathy wept
But she was too busy with her web.

II

A pebble in my mouth
If the pebble were a word
And my tissue-paper flesh and gauze tissues
Would fill so solidly this chair
The rose would ask
And even the oak
For a look at my menu
It would not have to be bread
It would not have to be meat
To turn their strong roots to a fable
It could be a pebble if it were a word

My teeth could seize
And my tongue know the substance and shape of.

A pebble in my mouth
If the pebble were a word
And my infant thoughts would stop their hungry
    crying
No poems for guard-rail
No chatter like this to bind them
In the crib of my skull
They would lie safe as lions
It would not have to be breasts
It need not be lollypops
To nourish and pacify them
It could be a pebble if it were a word
And a word could be tasted and sucked.

It would not have to be worms
It would not have to be seed
For me to trap at last the bird of my anguish
It could be a pebble and it would not have to deceive
Like the counterfeit fly of an angler
It would not have to be milk
It would not have to be a mouse
For my blood to purr
And my dying to vanish
It could be a pebble if it were a word
Not for the eyes and ears
But for the mouth.

III

On one of those nights
When the chipmunk is in his tunnel
Ah to crawl into the burrow
Of my own arteries—
Way down deep
Into my toes to creep
Like my own bones
Or the first gift that goes
Into a child's Christmas stocking . . . .
My own lymph to be—
To be my own pulse
To call on my own blood
My twin not my cousin
On one of those nights when the snow and the wind
Are the only ones out walking.

On one of those nights
When the birds have deserted Toronto
Ah to have a Morocco
By my mindless senses founded—
To take my soft breath
And fold it
Around my mind's chilly shoulders
To draw it up over my thoughts
To their very eyes
Like one of those costly wool blankets
The luxury shops advertise.

On one of those nights
When the chipmunk is in his burrow
And the squirrel stays home in his hollow
Ah to do this once—
One time!

IV

My poems flow over me
(Oh how could God be responsible
For man's sins
And rule from the moon
And look down on our ribs
When it's under oh always under
His writings and paintings and music
He lives?)

My poems flow over me
And fish of stone
How I envy the basketed minnows that writhe
On the sunny dry bank
Where your brown limbs stretch.

Others get warm at the fire
Loaned by the flint
Whose own flesh and soul
Are exiled from it
My poems flow over me
And chained like bare bone
To a sea-bottom throne
How I envy the dog that brings you your stick
And shakes off the water as I would shake off
Of art and poetry all talk
To lie on the dry shore near your breath.

V

I had the stakes
And the twine for the trellises
And the wire
I had the trowels and spades
I was ready to claim
Find a place in the sun for
And train
The weed in my blood with no name
I was ready
And it was not the wind that ferried
From my thighs to my brain
The cry in my veins
It was not the rain that carried
From my limbs to my palate
What slipped through my fingers and made
A fish of my pain.

I was the child again that on Halloween Eve
Stood with tied hands over the bobbing apples
But it was not a game I played
The basin was deep as the Carribean
And I knew the body a sea.

AH, BUT THE UNLOVED HAVE HAD POWER

W. H. Auden

On the dark water
When all the cities were drowned
I saw the white petal floating
And delicate still and whole as it floated
Over the mountains, and the towers
Of Edom and Babylon—
I saw your image held forever now
Safe in my brain as a child in its cradle
Though every building of my mind went down—

And I knew the love in the hearts of witches,
Of the Christs that are born with the dark hands of
    niggers,
And how on the wands of the black magicians
Cut from a tree with withered branches
The blighted blossoms return, as charms—
I knew how in squalor or age or vice or sickness
I could from any bed of lice or thorns,
If death turned snow to make your bed her arms,
Arise and with a touch of my soiled fingers
On your cold enbalming pillows,
Divert, a thousand years—perhaps a million,
The sun and thaw
God and the worms and angels
All were waiting for.

I, ONLY

Down on the road at the foot of the cliff
Noone would know a house was here
And who would be walking along that road
On so cold a night with everyone gone
From those other shacks this time of the year?

Why then do I lock my door
Bolted already . . . and hooked?
And tack to the windows to hide the lights
Anything thick enough?

Because of the fox with feet like a prayer
In fleeing me on the mountainside,
My arms full of brush?
Because of the buck
As timid still as the little hare
Though his horns are not in velvet now?
It cannot be the doe. And the bear
Will sleep as long as the crocus does—
It is man I fear.

Though noone would know
This hut was here
Except that fox and the hare and deer
It's a human step I think I hear
As I test the telephone . . .
It's a human hand with a knife and shears
And not the wind so sharp and strong
That is coming to cut the low wires down—
A hand like my own.

When my dog pricks up his ears
Is it my frozen bones he hears?
Do they creak as I play
(That shroud on the window panes and no sound
From my radio) the opposum's game?

It is not another dog
For he snarls
It is not another cat that scares
My cat as a pine branch falls—
I, only, have
Deep in my blood
And strong as love
Of my own kind the dread.

NEWS FROM OUR TOWN

He had not lived long in our town
But those who never knew him closely
Knew closely those who did
So that his death
Of the night before through every door
Had by the next night crept.

There was no dog whose bone
Lacked meat upon it no cat whose bowl
Lacked cream
And every lawn for days to come
Had crumbs for robins
And every ear long deaf
Heard how the sweetest bird of all
Sang when the sun had set.

Before one worm had brushed him
While still his limbs were neat
As seeds in packages
Out of his death that reached
So swiftly each home, there leaped
That marvelous flower of which each leaf
Is a human heart perfected . . .

Wives that had long been neglected
Had arms around them. The idler of our town
Had kind words said about him,
Our drunkard was defended
And letters unanswered from parents far away
Were suddenly remembered.

But he took his death
When they placed him underground
He took his death with him
He needed his death no doubt for his new living
And for the spinning
Of other flowers—
The first before a week had passed not having
One petal or one leaf unwithered
While every dog whose bone
Would tease *our* hunger and our women grown
Too fat or thin or old
For arms around them—
Oh all for whom our thrushes sing
Await now
Another death to mend it.

BEING TOUGH'S NOT EASY

I'd have loaned him that couple of bucks—
Poor Tom,
And being tough's not easy.
But you know how it is . . . he'd probably need
A dollar again tomorrow.

Ah Susie? We almost dropped in there today—
Just a block from the ward
During visiting hours . . .
But you know how it is—the pitiful way
She'd count on our coming again tomorrow.

Kind Jesus, withhold your touch,
Lest the palsy break out anew
After the resurrection dissolves
Your living hands to dew,

And Thy grace withhold, Oh Lord,
In this awkward disgraceful hour . . .
The weeds of love grown scrupulous
As never love's brief flower.

But death, oh grantest, Lord,
For death will last, thank God,
Till long after tomorrow.

MOVIE MARQUEE

With the magic of hands . . . of a lover's,
The words touch the skin . . .
Horror—Temptation—The Lusts of the East—
Terror—Rape—The Opium Dens—

The rivers swell in the veins again,
The senses' dry sea bottom with a sense of sin
Captures its waves and tides again.

But where does the géntle need come in?
Where is the woman who kissed Christ's hem
To find the whole world filled
With blooms and colors again?

No April was ever more bountiful . . .
Rape—Temptation—
New Orleans in Nineteen-ten—
The sap of the maple drips from the limbs,
The queues, in the snow, grow honey-bee wings.

But where are the radio listeners who write in
For *Sweet and Low* and *Emmy Lou*
And *I Will Take You Home, Kathleen?*

Where does the géntle need come in?

It is the cry locked in the rock,
And the rock must be melted in flames again.
It is the burr on the lion's fur,
And the lion must scatter the seeds again.

HOW THE RICH MOVE SOFTLY

How the rich move softly
Through their injustices,
Softly as the uncut grasses on summer noons they
    move—
That tinkle? It's their cocktail glasses,
That sound of hatchet blows?
I do not know,
For all is interstices
And open meadowland and willow laces
To their very gentle wickednesses
That knuckleless as summer breezes go.

So softly move the rich through their injustices,
Not softer is the breathing of a rose—
That tinkle's *not* the sound of glasses?
It's the bells then that the poor
Must sprout like antlers when too near
They venture to a rich man's loaves.
Those other sounds? That thump and clatter
As of a crutch on rugless stairs, and wooden shoes?
Those are the sins of the poor
Against the poorer still—
The rich's tread on moss with velvet soles,

And when the rich stretch out their arms
To grab and stab and kill,
You need not leave the tenement walls
Nor the asphalt walks to know
How easefully the purple hounds
That the delicate cream-puff clouds unloose
Do their dark hunting of the hillside's green—

So softly move
The rich through their injustices,
From Cairo to Tuckahoe
The jostling of daisies they carry
And the drift, on the white fields, of snow
That cover up and make so beautiful the cruelty
Of life from destruction deep below.

DEFENSE FACTORY

(Overtime Song)

Money
Money
Money money money
With the foxtrot skipped
As the waltz went swing
And the all-aboards shouted from a speeding
Non-stop train
As we clutched its wing
Oh who had time for the proper baggage?
But what do we need but our skins
In all this sunny sunny sunny
Suddeness of our prison chains
Yielding each link for a carousel ring?

Hurry
Hurry
Hurry hurry hurry
If you sweat enough
It's just like gin . . . .
Another and another and another
When they're pennies instead of a swig at Flynn's
And you don't need a hero's whoppers
Nor a crown and a throne like a king,
Nor a tie and shave and a movie star's ways
To get it without a marriage ring.

That the prices are high!
Oh it makes us feel richer
To fork up the cash
Without effort or flicker
For a sirloin done rare

When for coffee and air
We once had to pawn our tin tickers.
Quicker
Quicker
Quicker quicker quicker
Let the prices soar
(Ah, the war . . . the war!
It's hell *and* it's swell—
Like liquor!)

PAS DANS MON COEUR

Pas dans mon coeur . . .
It weeps on the slate
Of my brain and my brow,
And my marble cheek.
Pas sur la ville,
Except in one place,
Except on the tile
Of my long nights awake . . . .

Except on the granite winding sheet
That covers my life
Like love's embrace,.
Nowhere it rains
Nowhere it weeps.

Il ne pleure pas . . .
My heart has no fireplace;
Il ne pleut pas . . .
Too cold the town's dry streets.
But the rain of my love, oh my Love, how it beats
On my shroud of stone
Your absence makes.

LOVE SONG

I am the stone
Of the stone city

Their brokenness flows thróugh me
Who at the hour when the evening primrose folds
In sleep forever and the roaches crawl
Back to their cracks in tenement walls,
Can feel the factory whistle's call
Thrust in their eyeballs like a wedge
To pry their stuck lids open—
I am the granite of their city,
We die not singly,
From my melting flesh and bones
Lift them . . . new, and strong and whole,
As from the Ganges. Touch me.

Oh melt the stone
Of the stone city—
Their anguish fills me
Who when the wind and sleet are gone
That whipped their bodies upright
Wait till the dwindling breadlines form
Knowing there would be none at all
Were hallways strewn with pillows—
Kiss me,
That at the hour when in hospitals
The morgue fills fastest and the evening primrose
    folds
In sleep forever,
Back to his ancient meadows each may go,
His haystacks and his clover and his cows,
As I go home to you.

NEAR EVERY BED WHERE TWO SELVES MEET

Here, now,
Your life
Real and unknown
As the shapes in a Tanguy,

And there
Its body
Known and unreal
As rooms once lived in
Grown historic.
     Changed

To marble,
The headless lovely torso
Gives no token
Of crime or terror:

Only the severed living brain
Tells of the gold axe hung
Near every bed where two selves meet
To make of each not one.

TWO SONGS FROM "IN THE ASYLUM"

I

Speak to me
Test me
Prove I am deaf
Prove that the red on my tooth is blood
Prove that the hem of my dress came undone
So its thread could be drawn through my lips
Prove I am dumb as the deaf
Prove I can hear
The wonderful soundless speech underground
Where drowned kittens purr

Surround me with people
Keep me a year
In a big railway station
Inside the Bureau of Information
(I was alone
It was night
Noone would come
That's why I tried to cut off my tongue)
Talk to me
Test me
Prove that my lips are locked like God's ears
Prove that my ears are slow as His tears
Prove I am able to hear
The soundless virginal speech underground
Where cedars and bones confer

Some pray for temptations
For hunger and pain in unlimited rations
As strict make my trial but change
My Christ's nails to pebbles
To words hurled at me
Until from the *lamas*
Hosannas break free
For the needle piercing my lips
And the rose-leaves replacing my ears
Oh speak to me
Test me
Prove that again I shall hear
The speech of the voiceless underground
Before I lie there.

II

Hush let us whisper it
This is not Christmas yet
But continue to say
Merry Christmas
Continue to play it is Christmas Day
For we *must* be fooling someone

We *must* have enemies
There *must* be spirits we wish to deceive
Our priests must have told our chieftain
Of an eagle-eyed demon who hunts by day
At the sight of so much kindness
It *must* be that that is his favorite prey
We *must* be fooling someone
We *must* be hiding a gun
For the Evil One
Lured by this hoaxy benigness—

For the cleverest demon would hardly believe
These smiles and gifts and greetings
For every person in our clan
The bans and taboos all lifted
Rubies of glass
And pasted-on whiskers—

Even the cunningest couldn't conceive
Of the painted roasts on a picture-book page
Oozing real juices
And with real smells
Rounding up all the needy

We *must* have enemies
There *must* be spirits we wish to deceive
So continue to say Merry Christmas
Continue to play it is Christmas Day
But hush—say this low—
The real one is secret

FEMELLE DE L'HOMME

Return,
If only in a candle-lighted half dark glass,
The smoothness of her throat and brow;
Restore,
If only in a forest pool at sundown,
That look of youth male bark yields birdlime for,

And how that magic hat, invisibly
With rabbits filled,
That charmed her in her childhood will suddenly be
Some tattered schoolroom map of six by four
From which new Thurstons wonderfully draw
Real Aetnas
And all her prisons, whether bread or tears
The basins fill, again will have their doors
Past Vega, one, and one
Past Sirius—
Which, with the dwindling of her fanciers, are shrunk
To arm's reach, though more tight-locked than before.

No mind *called* mind is this
That, with a little finger, when
As sweet as trophies its bright fetterings,
Can fling
The farthest sky like curtain fluff
From God's most distant throne,
Then, gone the glitter with the keepers of
Its jail turned straw—can no more crawl
Than stones could, from the open cell
Where God sprawls too, now. Yet restore
To these remarkable as Phoenix wings
Their golden cage,
                   And see them soar.

I HAVE LET MYSELF BE PROVED

I have joined you, my love,
In abandoning me

In love that is not love
I have set myself free
But not from you
Only from me

I have let myself be proved
In love without love
Neither rib nor tree

Do you feel me near?
Or have I below
Left with my limbs under the snow
That contact of earth with the sky
The heart forgoes?

Do you feel me close
As a star to a star?
Do you feel me as near, Love,

And as far?

I have joined you
In abandoning me.

LOVE I MAKE IT BECAUSE I WRITE IT

It does not stay in the heart
It does not stay in the mind
(Ah, if it did, though . . . if . . .)
And when, the doors open and chafing against
Its narrow confines, forth it sets,
Oh what on those oceans where the clamorous flesh
Knows not the captain from the ship,
A lord still shall keep it . . .
The love untold and denied?
And what in the jungle of the thighs,
To the tiger, still a prince?
Love I make it because I write it
And as I say my darling, again from the skies
Athena alights at Odysseus's side.

Back on my book-shelves a hundred books of poems
Tell how the telling more than the knowing
Helpless as roses left the monsters
And all the enchanters dismayed
And quelled the waves, and saved,
While the glances thrown me
Down on the streets of my lonely roving
Change the story
To how on the tongues with a relish only
For the wine and honey a dollar buys
The word has died
That leaves with no crown and no shield and
    homeless and throneless
The trapped Ulysses-cry.

These lines I recall now:
"I am a woman, tell me lies,"

But where the caves are and those treacherous isles
And the cord of the gathered winds is untied,
The thrust is the same . . . . snatch the name,
And love I make it because I write it—
To find, as I say my darling,
The wax for the oarsmen again supplied
And the burning stick for the Cyclops-eye.